Bitcoin: Understanding Bitcoin, Mining, Investing & Trading for Beginners

Book #1 of the book series by Cryptomasher

Sean Bennett

Introduction Page

I want to thank you and congratulate you for purchasing the book,

"Bitcoin: Understanding Bitcoin, Mining, Investing & Trading for Beginners".

This book on the #1 cryptocurrency is intended for a complete novice. Written in a simple and easy-to-follow format, this is guaranteed to help you get your foothold in the complex world of the decentralized digital currency and set you ahead of the game.

Within the pages of this book, you will learn

- What is Bitcoin (BTC) and how Bitcoin came about
- What is blockchain technology
- What is Bitcoin wallet
- What is SegWit and the Lightning Network
- What is Bitcoin mining, mining pool
- What caused the Bitcoin Fork
- A brief overview about Bitcoin Cash (BCH/BCC)
- Bitcoin transactions for business

But that is not all! You will also learn

- How to earn Bitcoin
- How to secure your Bitcoins

- Tips for Bitcoin investing and Bitcoin trading with risk management techniques

- Various types of Bitcoin wallets as well as their Pros and Cons

- The uses of Bitcoin currency

- and much more!

Bitcoin has often be referred to as 'digital gold', as the blockchain technology allows to transfer value through software and software alone. Never before has it been possible to have trusted transactions directly between two or more parties that were authenticated by mass collaboration and powered by collective self-interests, instead of relying on large corporations motivated by profit.

Bitcoin continues to open new doors for anyone willing to invest and to do business, across the globe. Soon, Bitcoin may even become be the currency of every nation. We have tried to include the various aspects of Bitcoin in this book so that you can have a clear understanding about this huge societal breakthrough.

Thanks again for purchasing this book, I hope you enjoy it!

Contents

Bitcoin: Understanding Bitcoin, Mining, Investing & Trading for Beginners 1

Introduction Page 2

Chapter 1: Introduction and a Brief History of Bitcoin 6

Chapter 2: What is Blockchain Technology? 14

Chapter 3: Bitcoin Mining and Mining Pools 22

Chapter 4: What is SegWit and The Lightning Network? 29

Chapter 5: Bitcoin Wallet 35

Chapter 6: The Bitcoin Hard Fork 43

Chapter 7: Bitcoin Cash BCC/BCH 49

Chapter 8: Bitcoin Pricing from Launch to Now 53

Chapter 9: Investing in Bitcoin and Risk Management 56

Chapter 10: Bitcoin Trading 64

Chapter 11: The Security Aspect of Bitcoin 74

Chapter 12: Bitcoin Transactions for Business 81

Chapter 13: FOMO/FUD 83

Chapter 14: Dollar Cost Averaging 85

Chapter 15: Bitcoin Mutual Funds 87

Conclusion 89

© **Copyright 2017 by Cryptomasher - All rights reserved.**

This document is geared towards providing exact and reliable information in regards to the topic and issue covered. The publication is sold with the idea that the publisher is not required to render accounting, officially permitted, or otherwise, qualified services. If advice is necessary, legal or professional, a practiced individual in the profession should be ordered.

- From a Declaration of Principles which was accepted and approved equally by a Committee of the American Bar Association and a Committee of Publishers and Associations.

In no way is it legal to reproduce, duplicate, or transmit any part of this document in either electronic means or in printed format. Recording of this publication is strictly prohibited and any storage of this document is not allowed unless with written permission from the publisher. All rights reserved.

The information provided herein is stated to be truthful and consistent, in that any liability, in terms of inattention or otherwise, by any usage or abuse of any policies, processes, or directions contained within is the solitary and utter responsibility of the recipient reader. Under no circumstances will any legal responsibility or blame be held against the publisher for any reparation, damages, or monetary loss due to the information herein, either directly or indirectly.

Respective authors own all copyrights not held by the publisher.

The information herein is offered for informational purposes solely, and is universal as so. The presentation of the information is without contract or any type of guarantee assurance.

The trademarks that are used are without any consent, and the publication of the trademark is without permission or backing by the trademark owner. All trademarks and brands within this book are for clarifying purposes only and are the owned by the owners themselves, not affiliated with this document.

Chapter 1: Introduction and a Brief History of Bitcoin

What Is Covered In This Chapter?
What is Bitcoin?
The uses of Bitcoin
The history of Bitcoin

"Right now, Bitcoin feels like the internet before the browser" – Wenses Casares

Cryptocurrency, especially Bitcoin, has been clearly dominating the headlines in recent times. This comes as no surprise, as the returns from Bitcoin in the past year amounted to an unbelievable 668%!

According to the survey conducted by *Lend Edu*, the popularity of Bitcoin is growing steadily, especially among millennials. Nearly 87% of youngsters have heard about Bitcoin and are open to the concept of Bitcoin currency. While many wants to earn Bitcoin through Bitcoin mining, others prefer to make money via Bitcoin trading and Bitcoin investing.

If you are a complete newbie to Bitcoin and wish to gain an end-to-end knowledge about it in a *simplified* and *easy-to-understand* manner, I' ve got some great news. By reading this book, you are guaranteed to understand all the important aspects of Bitcoin, be it about Bitcoin wallet, Bitcoin trading, Bitcoin mining, Bitcoin investing, tips on how to earn Bitcoin (referred to as BTC), and more! This book is, quite simply, a one-stop reference for everything you want to know about Bitcoin.

However, be warned that Bitcoin is a complex topic that encompasses software engineering, cryptography, and economics. So, it may be tough for a non-technical person to grasp its intrinsic workings and programming aspects. Which is why I have covered the technical aspects of Bitcoin in a superficial manner in this book, without going too much into coding and programming details.

Now, let's get started with mastering Bitcoin!

Imagine that you have a bank account from which you send some money to another person, say, John. This is called a transaction wherein you send a fiat currency (Dollar) to another person. This transaction is authenticated and tracked by your bank and its record is maintained.

Note: Euro, Dollar, etc. are called fiat currencies due to a government decree ("fiat") declaring the currency to be legal tender.

But Bitcoin is a completely different ball game. Let's see why.

Understanding Bitcoin

Bitcoin is a peer-to-peer virtual currency without any central authority. This means that no bank, government, or official entity can issue or have control over Bitcoin. Whenever you send Bitcoin to someone else, it goes directly to them without any middlemen or banks.

Bitcoin is an open source code and exists through a cloud network known as the blockchain. The blockchain is basically a transparent ledger of all the transactions that ever happen on the Bitcoin network. Each and every transaction on Bitcoin network is authenticated by a collective network of the Bitcoin user's computers.

Bitcoin is pseudonymous. This means that Bitcoin can be used anonymously to an extent, as the sender and receiver are

Bitcoin

- Peer-to-peer virtual currency
- No central authority
- An open source code
- Exists though blockchain
- Is pseudonymous
- Payments happen instantly across the world
- Very nominal cost
- Common user interface to the Bitcoin system is Bitcoin wallet
- Transactions are secure as it uses strong cryptography
- Transactions are irreversible
- The final monetary base is fixed at 21 million Bitcoins

identified only by a string of numbers and alphabets. For example, 1pckXknnEd4SPkC27PnFH8dsY2gdGh26Y

Bitcoin payments are done using peer-to-peer technology. It happens instantly anywhere across the world for a very nominal cost.

Just like a web browser is a common user interface for the HTTP protocol, the common user interface to the Bitcoin system is called the 'Bitcoin wallet'. There are many Bitcoin wallets available, which is covered in detail in the upcoming pages. The transfer of value between Bitcoin wallets is called a transaction.

Bitcoin transactions are quite secure as it uses strong cryptography, making it impossible to be accessed without proper permission. The transactions of Bitcoin are irreversible. This helps in protecting users from fraudulent chargebacks.

The final monetary base of Bitcoin is fixed at 21 million Bitcoins. This scarcity provides the Bitcoins with value. The value of Bitcoin fluctuates based on the demand and supply.

Bitcoin ownership

The ownership of Bitcoin is established through Bitcoin addresses, digital keys, and digital signatures.

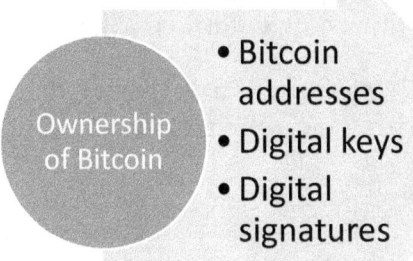

Keys come in pairs. There would be a private (secret) key and a public key. The digital keys are stored in the wallet.

The Bitcoin address is usually generated from and corresponds to the user's public key. Whenever Bitcoin transaction happens, the recipient's address would be the public key. Thus, public keys are used for receiving funds.

A valid digital signature is necessary for most Bitcoin transactions. It can only be generated with the secret key. The digital signature used to spend funds is also called a *witness*. Thus, the private key is required for spending funds as well as for signing transactions.

Next, let us see what Bitcoin is used for.

What is Bitcoin used for?

There are many uses of Bitcoin.

Bitcoin is used for transferring money by paying nominal fees.

Bitcoin is used as a payment option for goods and services. This includes real estate purchase, hotels, bars, air travel, gambling, e-commerce websites, technical services like VPN providers and hosting companies etc. The complete list of physical stores that accepts Bitcoin as payment can be found here.

Bitcoin can be converted to fiat currency and then spent as cash. This is done by withdrawing Bitcoin as cash from Bitcoin ATMs.

Many use Bitcoin for funding companies. Many donations are also accepted as Bitcoins.

Bitcoin is considered as a good idea for investment since it has been on a gravity-defying rise in the past years. Bitcoin trading is preferred by many investors due to its volatile nature.

Bitcoin can be used for purchasing gift cards and these gift cards can be used for buying products from online retailers.

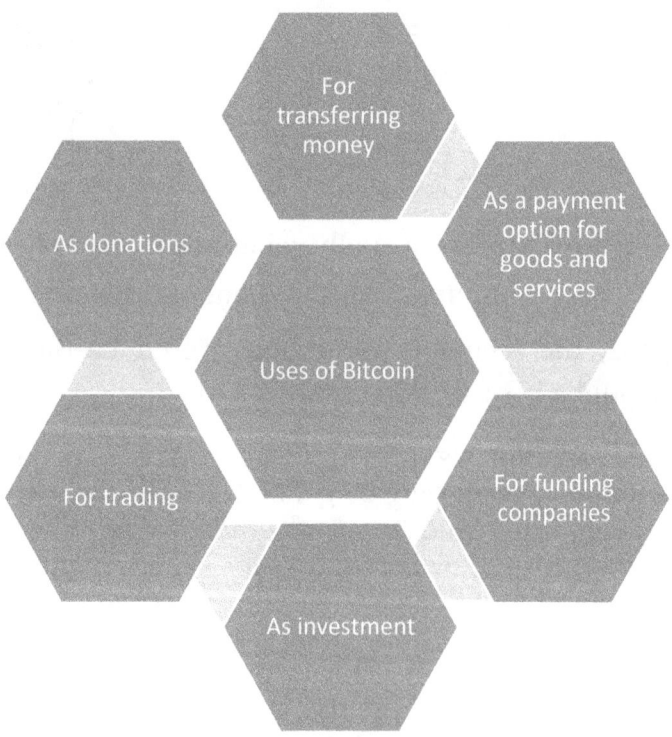

Now that you have a fair idea about the uses of Bitcoin, let us take a peek into its history.

The history of Bitcoin

The idea for Bitcoin was developed by someone called Satoshi Nakamoto. Interestingly, Satoshi Nakamoto is actually a pseudonym and the identity of the original developer remains a mystery.

In October 2008, Satoshi published a white paper, *Bitcoin: A Peer-to-Peer Electronic Cash System* via the Cryptography

History of Bitcoin

↓

Idea developed by Satoshi Nakamoto

↓

Satoshi published a white paper describing the overall idea behind Bitcoin on October 2008

↓

Satoshi developed the first software program to start mining

↓

Genesis block was mined by Satoshi in January 2009

↓

New version of code 0.2 released by Satoshi and larger group of developers

↓

The first Bitcoin transaction done for a physical good happened on 21 May 2010

↓

Bitcoin user Laszlo bought a $25 pizza for 10,000 Bitcoins.

Mailing List. The white paper described the overall idea behind Bitcoin and briefly touched on the major aspects of the system that Satoshi envisioned.

After publishing the paper, Satoshi developed the first software program to start *mining*, the name for the process of creating Bitcoin.

The first set of Bitcoin was mined by Satoshi in January 2009 and was named the *Genesis block*. Soon after, this project was announced to a group of cryptography experts.

By the start of 2010, a larger group of developers and Satoshi reviewed the code and released a new version of the code called 0.2 which improved the client.

Purchasing a pizza was the first Bitcoin transaction done for a physical good. This happened on 21 May 2010 when a Bitcoin user Laszlo bought a $25 pizza for 10,000 Bitcoins.

Chapter 2: What is Blockchain Technology?

What Is Covered In This Chapter?
What is a blockchain?
What are nodes, hash, and block?
Guarantees of blockchain
What is blockchain analysis?
What is the future of blockchain?

"Bitcoin will do to banks what email did to postal industry – Rick Falkvinge"

Before you can understand Bitcoin mining, Bitcoin trading, or learn about the ways to earn Bitcoin (BTC), it is important to know about blockchain technology. This is because once you learn about blockchain, you will know how the Bitcoin you send or receive is being tracked, learn the function of Bitcoin wallet in the process, and you can even plan your Bitcoin investing in a smarter way. Let's begin!

What is a blockchain?

The distributed database of Bitcoin is called a blockchain. It is basically a shared public digital ledger. It keeps a record of all the transactions that occur in the peer-to-peer network.

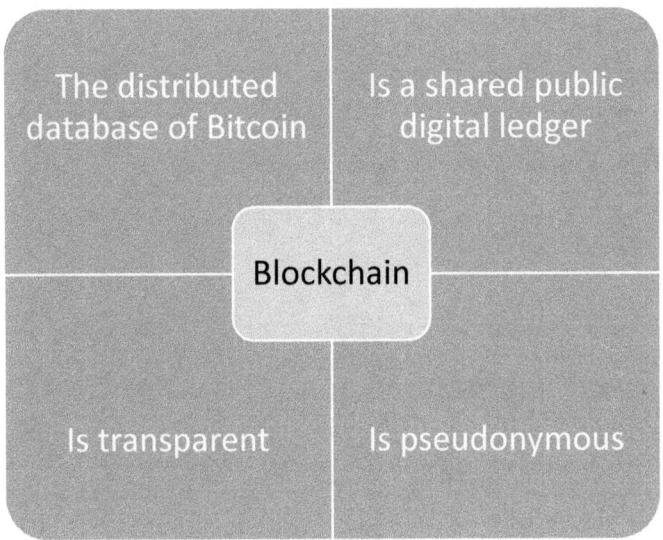

The blockchain can be stored as a flat file, or in a simple database. The Bitcoin blockchain is transparent, with the numbers and statistics fully disclosed.

The unprecedented transparency of Blockchain for the financial ecosystem is currently making many traditional financial institutions wary. But on the other hand, the pseudonymity associated with Bitcoin blockchain ensures that the companies or users are identifiable only via their Bitcoin wallet address and not by their real name or address.

Blocks

In a blockchain, the records are arranged in batches called *blocks*. The records within these blocks cannot be altered.

The blocks are a continuously growing list. Typically, the transactions are grouped in blocks of transactions every 10 minutes.

The blockchain database automatically updates itself as soon as any change happens.

The Bitcoin network blocks of the past cannot be altered because that would mean any block following that block number would need to be regenerated. Such a functionality is not available and is never planned to be made available.

Node

Blockchain database is distributed across many peer-to-peer networks of computers. These individual systems are called nodes.

Each Bitcoin node on the network will have a full copy of the entire transaction history of Bitcoin from 2009 till now.

As time goes on, many more transactions will get added to the current blockchain, thereby unveiling a timeline of how Bitcoin evolved.

Nodes are thus computers that constantly run the Bitcoin wallet software. Their function is to detect and validate new Bitcoin transactions.

```
┌─────────────────────────┐
│          Node           │
└─────────────────────────┘
             ↓
┌─────────────────────────┐
│ Each individual system  │
│ across which blockchain │
│ database is distributed │
│     is called a node    │
└─────────────────────────┘
             ↓
┌─────────────────────────┐
│ These computers constantly run │
│ the Bitcoin wallet software    │
└─────────────────────────┘
             ↓
┌─────────────────────────┐
│ Their function is to detect and │
│ validate new Bitcoin transactions. │
└─────────────────────────┘
```

For validating, updating, or retrieving any data, all the previous records can be easily obtained from the nodes. The validation done by the nodes occurs using some known algorithms.

Whenever someone requests a transaction, it is broadcast to the network of nodes for verification.

After the verification happens, the details of this transaction are encrypted and a new block is created for the ledger and added to the blockchain. The transaction is then deemed complete.

Hash

Each block identifies and references the previous block. This is done using something called a hash. It is a short, random sequence of letters and numbers.

Basically, every new block created after the original genesis block on the Bitcoin network contains a hash of the previous network block.

Each new block can be generated only in a chronological order since it contains the hash of a previous block. If not, the hash would be shown as unknown and the network will reject the block.

Ease of verification

Using the blockchain technology, the participants (sender and receiver) can transfer the assets without needing any centralized third-party verification. The decentralized nature of blockchain also gives it a major advantage, as it means there is no central point of failure that can bring down blockchain.

Unspent Transaction Outputs cache (UTXO)

The additional database kept by the nodes is called UTXO. This is a ledger which works as a cache for the blockchain.

UXTO consists of the record of funds available for each and every address. It is updated whenever there is a new transaction and funds get debited from the sending address and gets added to the receiving address.

Guarantees of Blockchain

The decentralized consensus algorithm avoids the issue of double-spend by ensuring that no UTXO can be spent twice.

The transaction data becomes immutable after recording a transaction in the blockchain and this is sufficient to work.

All the valid transactions get included in the blockchain at any time, irrespective of the origin or content, promoting neutrality.

The timestamp of the block can be trusted, giving an unspent-before guarantee. This is because the consensus rules reject any block if its timestamp is too far in the past or future.

The digital signatures offer authorization guarantees and are also validated in a decentralized network.

The transparency of transactions and availability in public makes it auditable. Every block and transaction can be traced to the genesis block.

Typically, Bitcoin value cannot be created or destroyed in any transaction, as the value of inputs is equal to the fees plus the value of outputs

The validity of the transaction stays unexpired as long as the consensus rules do not change and the inputs remain unspent.

Blockchain Analysis

Due to the transparent nature of blockchain, a new trend began to emerge called blockchain analysis.

In blockchain analysis, the industry experts perform detailed analytics on various aspects like how Bitcoins are spent, where are new wallets coming from, is there a hoarding problem, is the hoarding problem being addressed or escalating etc. These results are confidential and are provided only to the customers who request such intel.

Following are some results of blockchain analysis that are made available to the public.

- Median confirmation time for a transaction shows a somewhat exponential relationship with average transactions per block.
- Hash Rate and Difficulty level of the blockchain have a strong linear relation. A larger hash rate will result in the faster mining of blocks and the difficulty level will be set accordingly.
- Increase in the number of transactions within a block increases the block size, thereby requiring more time to validate it via proof of work and more time to propagate it over the network. This is known as impedance for a block.

There are also firms specializing in blockchain analysis. They provide customized reports for financial institutions, Bitcoin business, and cyber threat intelligence. Some of the solutions provided by such firms include:

- Following the traces of Bitcoin to find the services that cyber criminals are using to convert Bitcoin into cash or other digital currencies.
- Establishing connections between victims and estimate the revenues of criminals.
- Identifying criminal activity and determining the likely attack vectors facing the clients.
- Determining the source and destination of customer's Bitcoins to minimize the risk of doing business.
- Breaking down blockchain activity by different categories and assessing the risk of doing business with the client's customers.
- Providing due diligence tools that allow clients to visualize the source and destination of funds.
- Providing cyber threat intel.

The Future of Blockchain

The blockchain can be much more than a transaction ledger. There are currently many projects in development that will allow tools like smart contracts, copyright claims, and digital transfer of ownership etc. to exist on top of the blockchain.

Currently, there are applications and businesses that use the blockchain like *Barclays*, *Walmart*, and *Maersk*, the world's largest shipping company. *Everledger* is using blockchain technology to digitalize the features of diamonds, thereby tracking the stones' origins and authenticity as well as color and clarity.

Due to the transparent nature of blockchain, many financial services are focusing on developing blockchain applications. The underlying theme is to restore the actual power to the individual user without needing to rely on companies or centralized services. In fact, big banks are now planning to use blockchains to remake the SWIFT system, which is used for global interbank transfers.

Transparency and accountability is the need of the hour in the financial world, and blockchain seems to be the answer to that prayer.

Chapter 3: Bitcoin Mining and Mining Pools

What Is Covered In This Chapter?
What is Bitcoin mining?
What do miners do?
How are miners rewarded?
What is hash and proof-of-work?
What is a mining pool?

" The Bitcoin actually has the balance and incentives right and that is why it is starting to take off – Swwet Bitcoin."

By now, you would have understood how the Bitcoin transactions take place. Now the next logical question is, where does Bitcoin come from, originally? The short answer is that Bitcoins are generated by solving complex mathematical equations. Let's now understand how.

What is Bitcoin Mining?

Bitcoin mining serves mainly two significant purposes.

#1 It is the mechanism by which the security of Bitcoin is decentralized.

- Mining is the process of validating and storing the transaction information distributed within the Bitcoin network into the blockchain.
- Mining creates a secure, tamper-resistant consensus ecosystem for Bitcoin nodes to define whether the broadcasted transaction is valid or not valid. There should be at least a minimum of six network confirmations in order to deem a Bitcoin transaction spendable.

#2 It introduces new Bitcoin into the system

- Just like a central bank prints money and issues new notes, the money supply for Bitcoin is created through mining.

    At the end of the mining process, the new coin is generated. However, the reward is designed in such a manner to simulate diminishing returns, quite like the mining for precious metals.

What Do Miners Do?

Miners basically validate the new transactions and record them on the blockchain, which is the global ledger.

Every new block that contains transactions that happened since the last block is "mined" roughly every 10 minutes. These transactions are then added to the blockchain.

A transaction is said to be confirmed when it becomes a part of a block and is added to the blockchain. The recipient of the Bitcoin can spend the Bitcoin received only when the transaction is confirmed.

Purpose of Bitcoin Mining
- Is the mechanism by which the security of Bitcoin is decentralized
- Introduces new Bitcoin into the system

However, all this requires a significant amount of computing power. So, why exactly do users do it? The answer is: because they are rewarded.

How Are Miners Rewarded?

In exchange for the security provided by the miners, they get two types of rewards.

#1 *The transaction fees from all the transactions that are verified and included in the block.*

- Each transaction typically includes a transaction fee. This is received in the form of a surplus of Bitcoin between the inputs and outputs of the transaction.
- The winning Bitcoin miner will be able to get the surplus Bitcoin on the transactions included in the winning block.

#2 *The new coins created with each new block are known as Block Rewards.*

- The maximum amount of newly created Bitcoin that a miner can get from a block is programmed to be halved every 4 years (every 210,000 blocks).
- In January of 2009, the reward was at 50 Bitcoin per block. This was then halved to 25 Bitcoin per block in November of 2012. In July 2016, the reward was halved again to 12.5 Bitcoin.
- Going by the same formula, the rewards decrease exponentially until the year 2140 after which no more new Bitcoin will be issued and almost all the Bitcoin (20.99999998 million) will have been issued.

But this whole process is not as simple as it sounds. This is because there are many Bitcoin miners on the network and only the winner gets the reward. Miners compete with each other to be the first one to correctly solve some specialized math problems in order to assemble the outstanding transactions into a block.

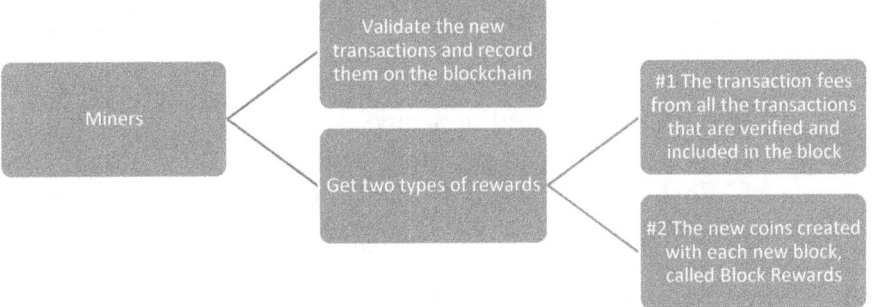

For making the final decision on which block of the transaction should be entered into the blockchain, the miners will have to provide something called proof-of-work.

What is Proof-Of-Work?

- In order to win the reward, miners should first take the information of a Bitcoin block and verify its integrity.
- Once done, they apply a complicated mathematical formula to this block of Bitcoin data.
- Once this formula is applied, a new block will be formed which consists of shorter, seemingly random sequences of letters and numbers, known as a hash.
- Hash is basically a difficult math formula based on a cryptographic hash algorithm called SHA-256 algorithm.
- All miners try and solve this mathematical formula to calculate a block's hash.
- In order to successfully do that, the miner needs to hash the block's header so that it is less than or equal to the target value provided. For example, the target value could be given as '256-bit alphanumeric string that starts with 18 zeros'. The target value of hash varies every 2016 blocks to keep things more difficult.
- Interestingly, you can't actually solve this logically – you have to speculate the answer. You can think of it like trying to guess the combination for the lock.

- So, miners try to arrive at the target (hash) by varying a small portion of the block's headers, which is called a "nonce." The miner attempts many times to solve the formula by varying the nonce.
- The solution to the problem is referred to as the Proof-of-Work since a large amount of work is carried out in order to mine the block successfully.

As soon as the hash is solved, it gets stored on the Bitcoin blockchain along with the block that it was derived from, thereby acting as proof that the miner expended significant computing effort.

Whichever miner obtains the correct Bitcoin Hash first will win the lottery and get the block reward of 12.5 BTC. The computational power of miners measured in hashes/second is called hash rate. The network hash rate is the total hash rate of all the miners in the network

Mining Technology

As the popularity of Bitcoin surged, the mining technology also improved, leading to the manufacturing of state-of-the-art chips. The mining has proceeded from using Central Processing Unit (CPUs), Graphics Processing Unit (GPUs), and Field-Programmable Gate Array (FPGAs) to Application Specific Integrated Circuit (ASICs). Each new iteration of chips has made mining easier.

Now, anyone can participate in Bitcoin mining by running a computer program. However, as the environment grew to be more competitive, individual miners working alone lost out slowly to the growing commercial systems.

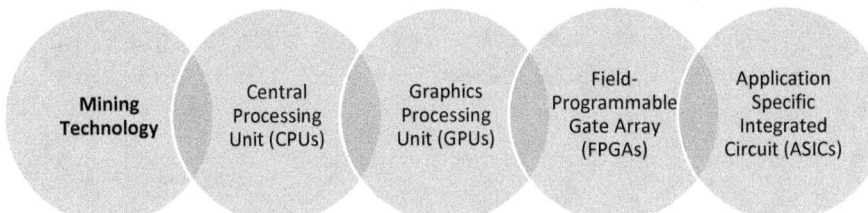

In fact, as the mining difficulty increased, miners holding the older hardware like CPUs and GPUs are slowly moving to mine other cryptocurrencies.

This lead to the concept of the 'Mining Pool'

What is a Mining Pool?

Instead of trying to mine Bitcoin individually, miners now collaborate in order to form mining pools. In a mining pool, thousands of participants basically pool their hashing power and then share the reward among themselves.

Although each miner gets a smaller share of the overall reward by participating in a pool, the positive is that they typically get rewarded every day, reducing uncertainty. There are specialized pool-mining protocols for coordinating the mining pools. Here's how it works.

- Each individual miner will first create an account with the pool and then configure his or her mining equipment to connect to the pool server.
- While mining, their mining hardware remains connected to the pool server synchronizing their efforts with the other miners.
- So, the pool miners share the effort to mine a block and then share in the rewards.
- The reward is paid to a pool Bitcoin address initially. After the rewards reach a specific threshold, the pool server makes payments to the miners' Bitcoin addresses.
- A percentage fee of the rewards is charged by the pool server for providing the pool-mining service.

Mining pools are open to any miner irrespective of whether they are big or small. Some miners may have a single small mining machine, and others may possess a houseful of high-end mining hardware.

Chapter 4: What is SegWit and The Lightning Network?

> **What Is Covered In This Chapter?**
>
> **What is SegWit?**
>
> **Benefits of SegWit**
>
> **What is the Lighting Network?**

"We have elected to put our money and faith in a mathematical framework that is free of politics and human error. – Tyler Winklwvoss"

As Bitcoin grew bigger, it faced mainly three challenges.

- Network congestion
- Increased time for verifying transactions
- Higher transaction fees

Hence, it became imperative for the platform to get faster and more scalable. Before we go into details about how to do that, let us understand a little bit more about a typical Bitcoin block.

Understanding the Bitcoin Block

Cryptocurrencies and blockchains are essentially built out of blocks. Within the block, there are different layers of data. With the Bitcoin blockchain, each block had a limit of 1 MB.

This was done by Satoshi because they foresaw a possible DoS attack (denial of service attack) on the blockchain. He feared that hackers and trolls would stuff the blocks with spam transactions and mine blocks which could be unnecessarily big in order to clog up the system.

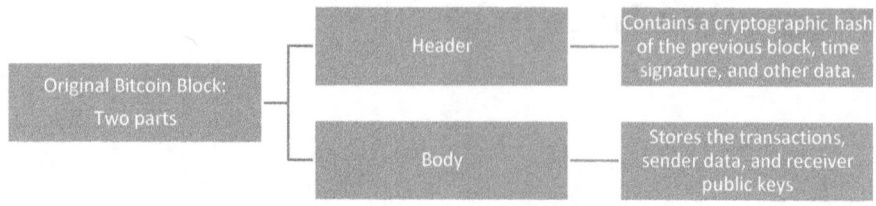

A block consists of two parts: a header and a body. The header contains a cryptographic hash of the previous block, time signature, and other data. The body stores the transactions, sender data, and receiver public keys. These help to ensure that these are legitimate transactions

One of the solutions proposed for overcoming the challenges of Bitcoin is the Segregated Witness (SegWit).

What is Segregated Witness (SegWit)?

SegWit is a software upgrade of Bitcoin proposed by the Bitcoin Core development team in 2016. It is a soft fork, meaning that it is backward-compatible.

SegWit protocol breaks down the original block into two parts, the original block and an extended "witness" block.

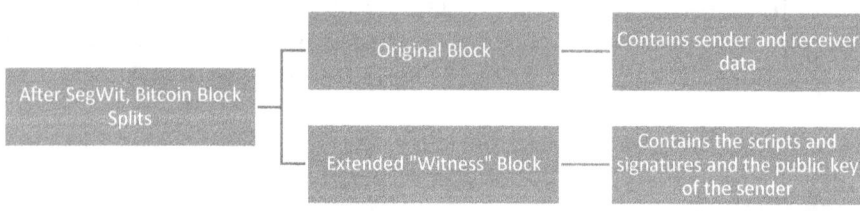

The original section retains the sender and receiver data. SegWit removes the script or code from the transactions and puts it into an extended block. This means that the new

"witness" segment contains the scripts and signatures and the public key of the sender.

After SegWit upgrade, more vacant space gets created in the original block. So, the block size would remain the same, but it can contain data more efficiently.

Bitcoin split into Bitcoin (BTC) and Bitcoin Cash (BCC or BCH) on August 1, 2017. In the Bitcoin (BTC) network, the SegWit changes were successfully implemented.

What Are The Advantages of SegWit?

SegWit improves the efficiency, thus enabling transactions to be confirmed faster. This helped in curbing the relatively higher transaction fees which happened due to increased demand.

SegWit fixes transaction malleability as the malleable parts of the transaction is now moved to the segregated witness.

SegWit changes the calculation of the transaction hash for signatures in such a way that each byte of a transaction only needs to be hashed at most twice. This means that large transactions can be generated without running into problems due to signature hashing. This also makes it easier to increase the block size.

It benefits hardware wallet manufacturers as SegWit explicitly hash the input value. SegWit helps in reducing the Unspent Transaction Output (UTXO) database growth. SegWit also laid the groundwork for a "Lightning Network", wherein the transactions are cheaper, more scalable, and faster.

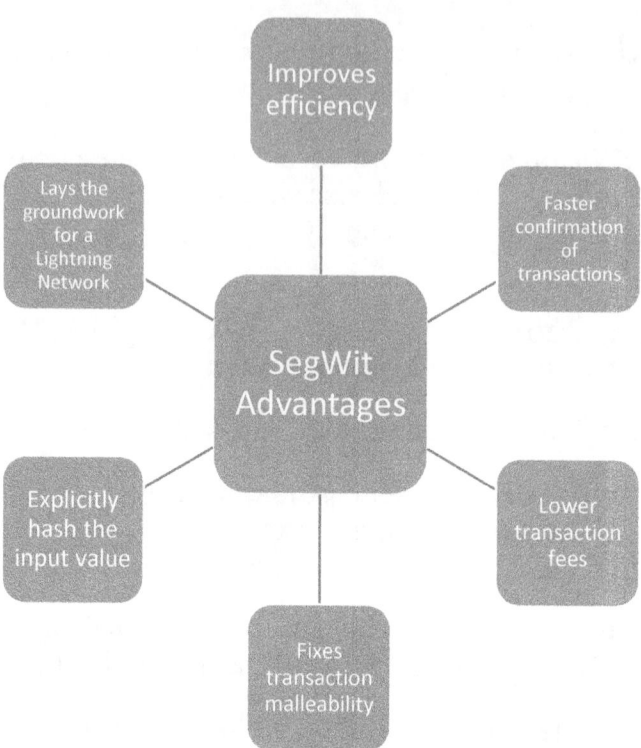

What is The Lightning Network?

The Lightning Network is a routed network of bidirectional micro-payment system that is connected end-to-end. It was described by Joseph Poon and Thadeus Dryja in February 2015 initially. This system provides a mechanism for users to execute smart contracts on the blockchain itself.

Lightning networks help in establishing near-instant micropayments from channel to channel. This can be done without needing to trust any of the intermediaries or offloading transactions to a custodian which would have required fee payments higher than the transaction amount. Users will be able to send amounts as little as 0.00000001 BTC through time-lock and hash-lock mechanisms and a trust-less system.

The bi-directional payment channels allow payments to be securely routed across multiple peer-to-peer payment channels. Any peer on the network can pay any other peer even if they don't directly have a channel open between each other. The transactions can be committed while broadcasting to the rest of the Blockchain at a later time.

The Lightning Network effectively makes Bitcoin Scaling possible by conducting such transactions off-chain using Bitcoin scripting, with enforcement done through broadcasting signed multi-signature transactions on the blockchain itself.

The developers of the network have indicated that its speed would enable it to "be used at retail point-of-sale terminals, with user device-to-device transactions or anywhere instant payments are needed."

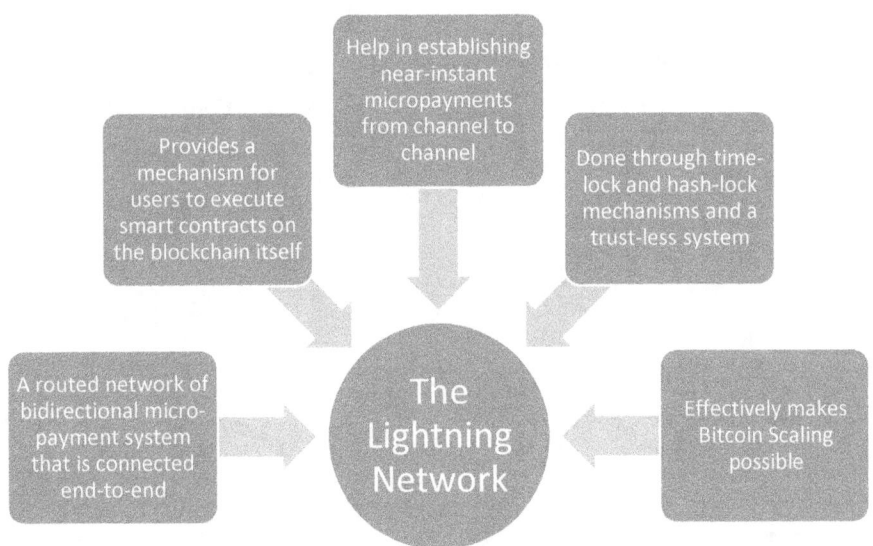

The Lightning Network uses SegWit as purely SegWit transactions are not vulnerable to transaction malleability. This means that the transaction ID for such a transaction cannot change thereby helping the Lightning Network to work much better.

How Does The Lightning Network Work?

- First, the participants should agree to transact on a separate, offline channel.
- Funds are then placed into this two-party, multisignature "channel" Bitcoin address. This channel is represented as an entry in the Bitcoin public ledger.
- Both parties must agree on the new balance for spending the funds from the channel.
- The current balance is stored as the most recent transaction signed by both parties, spending from the channel address.
- To make a payment, both parties sign a new exit transaction spending from the channel address. All old exit transactions are invalidated by doing so.
- The middleman of the mining rig or digital wallet provider could be skipped entirely.

Chapter 5: Bitcoin Wallet

> *What Is Covered In This Chapter?*
>
> **What is a Bitcoin wallet?**
>
> **What are the tasks performed by Bitcoin wallet?**
>
> **What are the types of Bitcoin wallets?**

"You can't stop things like Bitcoin. It will be everywhere and the world will have to readjust. World governments will have to readjust" - John McAfee

Just like you need a bank account to send or receive funds, you need something called a Bitcoin wallet for sending and receiving your Bitcoins. Interestingly, unlike the traditional wallets, digital wallets don′t store currency. Let′s now learn more about Bitcoin wallets.

What Is A Bitcoin Wallet?

A Bitcoin wallet is basically a software program. Just like you need an email program like Gmail to manage your emails, a Bitcoin wallet is necessary for managing your Bitcoins. A Bitcoin wallet stores a collection of your Bitcoin private keys and public keys.

The wallet interfaces with blockchain so that you can send and receive money as well as monitor your balance. Overall, it acts as a personal ledger of transactions. A wallet is protected from unauthorized access and is usually encrypted with a password.

Bitcoin wallet
- Stores a collection of your Bitcoin private keys and public keys
- Interfaces with blockchain so that you can send and receive money as well as monitor your balance
- Is protected from unauthorized access and is usually encrypted with a password

As soon as you install the Bitcoin wallet software, you will be presented with a Bitcoin wallet address. This serves as the identification number by which you will be known as a member of the Bitcoin network. This can be compared to your bank account number. Your Bitcoin balance is associated with the Bitcoin address.

The private key allows you to spend Bitcoins from that address. The private key is represented either as a string of letters and numbers or as a QR code.

What Are The Functions Performed By A Bitcoin Wallet?

A Bitcoin wallet is basically a service that collects all of your public addresses into one place. Some of the important tasks performed by the wallet software are

- Querying the blockchain and letting the user know the total available funds.
- Generating new addresses for receiving new funds or change from transactions performed by the wallet software.
- Generating or reading QR codes that represent addresses, transactions, etc.
- Sending funds to the address chosen by the user.
- Tracking the confirmation status of transactions and publishing the transaction to the blockchain.
- Creating the backup of the wallet and restoring the backup as requested by the user.

What Are The Types Of Wallets?

There are mainly two categories of Bitcoin wallets. They are Hot wallet and Cold storage wallet.

Any Bitcoin wallet that is online and connected to the internet in some way is called a hot wallet. When Bitcoin private keys are created and stored in a secure offline environment, it is called a cold storage wallet. Every type of Bitcoin wallet comes under one of these categories.

There are mainly four different types of wallets. They are

1. Online or Web Wallets
2. Software Wallets
3. Hardware Wallets
4. Paper Wallets

#1 *Online Wallets or Web Wallets*

This type of wallet can be accessed from any device that has internet connectivity. They are basically applications or websites that are responsible for the management of private keys. Online wallets belong to the category of *hot wallets*.

Some examples of online wallets are *Blockchain.info, Bitgo, Coinbase.com, GreenAddress* etc.

<u>Advantages of Online/ Web Wallets</u>

- ☑ Can be accessed from any device that has internet connectivity
- ☑ Is easy to setup
- ☑ They are usually linked with cryptocurrency exchanges or Bitcoin exchanges online
- ☑ Ease of use

<u>Disadvantages of Online/ Web Wallets</u>

- ☒ The application of the website will have control over your Bitcoin
- ☒ The private keys have to be saved on someone else's server
- ☒ The app or website management can suspend or limit your account anytime for any reason
- ☒ Is more prone to hackers

- ☒ Possibility of technical glitches

#2 Software Wallets

There are two types of software wallets – desktop wallets and mobile wallets. A software wallet is designed to be downloaded and used on personal computers, smartphones, and laptops. So, a software wallet is basically an application that is installed on the user's system, desktop computer, or mobile. Software wallets can be accessed easily and can be used even when the device does not have internet connectivity.

Mobile wallets are a less-secure option compared to other wallets. This is because instead of running a full Bitcoin client, Simplified Payment Verification (SPV) is used on the mobile device. Hence, mobile wallets are usually recommended for the storage of a limited number of Bitcoins only. Software wallets belong to the category of *hot wallets*.

Some examples of the desktop wallet are *Bitcoin core, Multibit, Armory, Electrum.org* etc. Some examples of the mobile wallet are *Wirex, Mycelium, Xapo, Bitcoin Wallet (blackberry), Bread wallet* etc.

<u>Advantages of Software Wallets</u>

- ☑ You have the control over your Bitcoin, not a third party website.
- ☑ There is better security compared to the online wallets
- ☑ The data is available on the user's mobile device or computer.
- ☑ It is easier to back-up by yourself

<u>Disadvantages of Software Wallets</u>

- ☒ You must have some technical knowledge for using software wallet.
- ☒ It is easier for hackers to hack your mobile device or computer and gain access to your wallet using malware.

☒ If you lose your device, your wallet is also lost.

#3 Hardware Wallets

Hardware wallets are usually USB shaped devices. These devices store private keys and sign transactions with these private keys.

Hardware wallets communicate with a client's wallet software in the computer. Transactions are sent to the hardware wallet from the client wallet on the computer through the USB connection.

The client acts as an intermediary between the blockchain and the hardware wallet and transmits the transactions signed inside the hardware wallet.

Hardware wallets typically have a small display screen that shows information about the transaction. There are also some buttons provided for allowing the user to decide whether to approve or decline the transaction. This is intended as an added security against malware attacks which would modify the transaction details. So, by simply declining the transactions, the user can avoid such hacks.

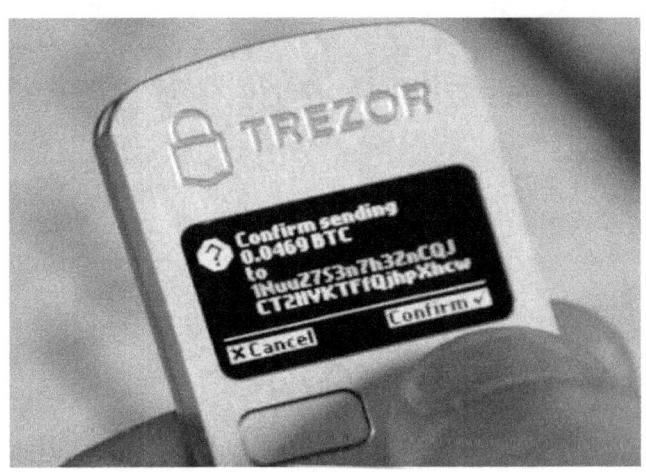

There is usually a PIN or password required for accepting the transactions that come through the connection.

For sending Bitcoin, you just need to plug in your device to any internet-enabled computer or device, enter a pin and then send Bitcoin and confirm. Then, it can be taken offline for transportation and security.

Hardware wallets belong to the category of *cold storage wallets*. Most hardware wallets provide a seed backup in case that the device itself is lost or stolen.

Some examples of hardware wallet are *Keepkey, Ledger, and Trezor* etc.

<u>Advantages of Hardware Wallets</u>

- ☑ Is one of the most secure wallets available
- ☑ Is it possible to have backups
- ☑ It is password protected
- ☑ There is a lower risk of malware based hack attempts

<u>Disadvantages of Hardware Wallets</u>

- ☒ They have to be taken care physically.
- ☒ Is very small in size and can be lost if not careful.
- ☒ They are not free.

#4 Paper Wallets

Paper wallets are one of the easiest wallets to use. These wallets are a physical copy or print out of the QR code of your Bitcoin public and private keys on a paper.

Once the printed keys are available, you can simply use them wherever you want just by adding public-private key combination into your existing wallet service. Paper wallets belong to the category of *cold storage wallets*.

Paper wallets can be easily generated using a tool. An example is the client-side JavaScript generator at *bitaddress.org*.

Advantages of Paper Wallets

- ☑ Gives you more control on your wallet.
- ☑ Has better security than online and software wallets.
- ☑ It can be stored and taken care of even when there is no internet connection.
- ☑ You do not need to hold it onto a computer or mobile device

Disadvantages of Paper Wallets

- ☒ The possibility of theft as it is stored physically, especially if there are multiple copies.
- ☒ As it is a paper, it can get faded or damaged with time.
- ☒ Technical know-how is required for generating and using a paper wallet.

Quick Tip: Which type of Bitcoin wallet is Best Suited for You?

Now that you have learned about the different types of wallets and their pros and cons, here is a quick overview about which wallet suits you best based on what you need it for.

- ♦ For small, yet frequent transactions: Online wallets or Software wallets

- For Cryptocurrency exchange: Online wallet
- For occasional big transactions: Hardware wallet
- Only for Storage: Paper wallet or Hardware wallet

Chapter 6: The Bitcoin Hard Fork

> ***What Is Covered In This Chapter?***
>
> **What is the Bitcoin civil war?**
>
> **What was Satoshi's vision?**
>
> **Scaling solution: SegWit vs Big Blockers**
>
> **Why did Bitcoin split into two?**
>
> **After the fork**
>
> **Quick overview: BTC vs BCH**
>
> **What is SegWit2X?**
>
> **What is Bitcoin Gold?**

"Bitcoin is not a currency for a government, it is a global currency for the people." – Wenses Casares

After a long drawn out battle that lasted more than two years over the rules that should guide the cryptocurrency's network, Bitcoin underwent a hard fork. On 1st August 2017, the digital currency Bitcoin split into two derivative currencies

- Bitcoin (BTC)
- Bitcoin Cash (BCH/ BCC)

What Is The Bitcoin Civil War?

It all started in 2010 when a spam control measure of 1 MB per 10-minute limit was added to the codebase of Bitcoin. This was added because the value of Bitcoin was just a few cents and the developers did not want attackers to overload the network with a large number of cheap transactions.

But within a few years, Bitcoin saw an unprecedented growth and Bitcoin found itself unable to absorb this increased demand. Every transaction started happening at the expense of another, leading to a fee bidding war. This, in turn, resulted in a steep rise in the transaction fee. The transaction fees surged from just a few pennies to almost $5 by mid-2017.

Bitcoin's growing adoption and use were slowly on the verge to be threatened. Yet, the community could not agree on the two scaling solutions that were proposed. This was nicknamed as the 'Bitcoin Civil War'.

What Did Satoshi Envision?

When the original Bitcoin was created by Satoshi, he envisioned a network wherein each person would run a node. Each of the nodes would hold the entire blockchain and serve the peers. This way, the blockchain would remain immutable and not under the control of a single entity.

However, the size of blockchain grew rapidly over the years, making it impossible for a regular computer to run a full node. It needed bigger storage space as well as higher bandwidth for the internet. Thus, the volunteer nodes also started to decline slowly.

Meanwhile, people had to wait till the creation of new blocks so that their transactions would go through. This created a backlog of transactions. It had finally lead to a situation wherein the only way to get your transactions through was to pay a high enough transaction fee. Such fees would attract and incentivize the miners to prioritize the transaction.

The Two Scaling Solutions: Big Blockers vs SegWit

There were two scaling solutions – big blockers and SegWit.

- ***Big Blockers:*** The big blockers put forward a simple solution - increase the block size. If each block can hold more data, then the network can process more transactions per second.
  The drawback is that as the block size increases, the blockchain also grows bigger. Bigger blockchain would also

lead to fewer nodes, implying less decentralization. This is because not many can afford the high expense required for the storage of that much amount of data.
- ***SegWit:*** Team SegWit advocated for a sophisticated kind of data compression that would allow transaction data and signatures to be split. The signatures could then be compressed so that more transactions could fit into the regular 1 MB blocks.
  The compression would lead to a smaller blockchain, which would lead to more nodes hosting it.

Why Did Bitcoin Split Into Two?

As the scalability debate raged on, the community became divided into two camps.

- Those who supported the big blockers. They preferred to have larger blocks which could, in turn, hold more transactions.
- Those who supported the SegWit solution. This camp favored a more technically nuanced solution.

Both camps were not ready for a compromise. It eventually ended with the #1 cryptocurrency splitting into two – BCC and BTC.

After the Hard Fork

Assume that you owned 1 Bitcoin before the split. Then, post-split, you would own 2 Bitcoins – one coin on the original Bitcoin network, and a second coin on the new Bitcoin Cash network. The 2 coins have almost the same cryptographic credentials, but their prices vary.

All past transactions on Bitcoin Cash' s new blockchain is identical to Bitcoin core' s blockchain while future transactions and balances are totally independent of each other for Bitcoin and Bitcoin Cash.

BTC vs BCH/BCC

BTC: The Bitcoin Classic chain retained the 1 MB limit and the legacy ticker symbol, BTC. It activated a transaction malleability fix and scaling solution called Segregated Witness (SegWit) protocol. The block size limit on a blockchain was increased by removing signature data from Bitcoin transactions.

BCC/BCH: The Bitcoin Cash chain increased the limit to 8 MB and adopted a new ticker symbol, BCH (or BCC).

The Debate of SegWit2X

When the software upgrade called Segregated Witness (SegWit) was proposed, it comprised of two phases – SegWit and SegWit2X.

During the first phase, SegWit, in August 2017, the transaction data was planned to be moved outside of the block on a parallel track. During the second phase, SegWit2X, in November 2017, the Bitcoin's block size was planned to be increased.

The second phase of the process, SegWit2X, would have actually been an upgrade to the current codebase of Bitcoin. SegWit2X proposed to allow block sizes that are larger than 2MB (to even 8MB). However, this required a 92% agreement.

Not everyone supported this hard fork. There was even a "No2X" social media movement pushing to reject the November implementation. Following were the main reasons for the lack of support for SegWit2X

SegWit2x was designed in such a way that the software would activate even if just 1 percent of the community supported it, which would lead to another split.

The development team, led by Bloq CEO Jeff Garzik, had refused to implement a feature called replay protection.

Some miners have already embraced Bitcoin Cash and see the SegWit2x proposal was an unnecessary and unloved alternative.

The Outcome?

The outcome of the SegWit2X debate was that the upgrade and any fork was cancelled. The Bitcoin community failed to reach a consensus and the miners pushing for the upgrade gave in to the traders.

"Our goal has always been a smooth upgrade for Bitcoin... Unfortunately, it is clear that we have not built sufficient consensus for a clean blocksize upgrade at this time. Continuing on the current path could divide the community and be a setback to Bitcoin's growth."   - Mike Belshe, BitGo CEO

If the upgrade did go ahead the fork could have lead to a contentious hard fork of Bitcoin into SegWit and SegWit2X, which would have been two incompatible blockchains and currencies. After the split, if Bitcoin remains as the majority blockchain, SegWit2x would have operated under a different moniker to BTC and Bitcoin. On the flip side, if SegWit2x turned out to be the majority chain, the BTC and Bitcoin moniker would have been used to support the SegWit2x chain.

The abandoning of the fork is a testament to the confidence in the network behind Bitcoin as laid down by Satoshi.

Bitcoin Gold Hard Fork

On 24th October 2017, yet another fork happened to Bitcoin from block 491,407 called Bitcoin Gold (BTG). Bitcoin Gold fork was not formed to find a solution for Bitcoin's scaling problem, but to re-decentralize the mining of Bitcoin and return power to independent miners.

Bitcoin Gold was formed due to two main reasons.

- To change how mining works by making it so the most powerful mining machines (called ASICs) can no longer be used. The forked Bitcoin Gold system will, therefore, use a different "proof-of-work" block-verification algorithm.
- To attract more people to this system over time and free the Bitcoin network from the large companies who 'command undue influence on the network'.

While exchanges like Bittrex declined to list Bitcoin Gold (BCG) trading, others like Japan's bitFlyer have declared their support for BCG. Nicknamed as the people's fork, Bitcoin Gold allows miners to mine Bitcoin with GPUs.

The bottom-line is that this has created yet another alternate version of Bitcoin. Overall, it seems as though we may have four competing versions of Bitcoin by the beginning of December. They are, Bitcoin SegWit, Bitcoin Cash, Bitcoin SegWit2X, and Bitcoin Gold. We will have to see which one deems to be the most lucrative. As of writing this book, Bitcoin is still the most valuable.

Chapter 7: Bitcoin Cash BCC/BCH

> **What Is Covered In This Chapter?**
>
> What is Bitcoin Cash?
>
> Features of BCC
>
> Why BCC is against SegWit?

"I think Bitcoin is a technical tour de force" – Bill Gates

Let us now learn more about the new entrant – Bitcoin Cash (BCC/BCH).

What is Bitcoin Cash?

Bitcoin Cash was proposed by the miners and developers of Bitcoin who were concerned with the future of the cryptocurrency and its ability to scale effectively.

Bitcoin Cash website defines it as follows: *Bitcoin Cash is a peer-to-peer electronic cash for the Internet. It is fully decentralized, with no central bank and requires no trusted third parties to operate.*

Bitcoin Cash is represented by the ticker symbols BCC or BCH depending on the service or wallet. XBC is also used to meet the International Standard for currency codes (ISO 4217).

Why Not SegWit?

The big blockers (Bitcoin Cash supporters) disagreed with the SegWit Proposal as they felt that it had a few drawbacks.

As the block size remains 1 MB, the miners will get only lesser transaction fees for each individual transaction. SegWit implementation, a complex procedure, had to be done by all the wallets by themselves. It was probable that many things could go wrong in the implementation. The increase in the capacity, transactions, bandwidth etc. will significantly increase the usage of resources as well.

The big blockers also believed that SegWit solution did not address the fundamental problem of scalability in a meaningful way and would not be able to handle exponential growth or worldwide usage, SegWit did not follow the roadmap initially outlined by Satoshi Nakamoto, SegWit2x, which was introduced as the road forward lacked transparency, SegWit introduction undermined the decentralization and democratization of the currency, and SegWit implementation's discardable signatures would weaken Bitcoin's security model.

Features of BCC/BCH

Bitcoin Cash is basically a fork of the Bitcoin blockchain ledger with upgraded consensus rules. After the August 1 split, all Bitcoin holders as of block 478558 are also owners of Bitcoin Cash.

Bitcoin Cash is quite similar to Bitcoin, but there are some major differences between the two. Following are the features of Bitcoin Cash.

Features of Bitcoin Cash

- Has a block size of 8 MB
- Allows nearly two million transactions to be processed per day
- Has no SegWit protocol
- Has no "replace by fee" feature
- Has a feature called replay and wipeout protection which prevents replay attacks using a redefined sighash algorithm
- Can adjust the proof-of-work difficulty quicker than Bitcoin due to EDA

Bitcoin Cash has a block size of 8 MB. This allows nearly two million transactions to be processed per day. Research is currently underway to allow for huge future increases. There would be no SegWit protocol in Bitcoin Cash.

The "replace by fee" feature would not be available in Bitcoin Cash. In Bitcoin, it is possible to overwrite the previous transaction and make it null and void by adding another transaction with high enough fees to incentivize miners and let the transaction go through. This is called 'replace by fee'.

Bitcoin Cash will have a feature called 'replay and wipeout protection.' A replay attack is a data transmission that is maliciously repeated or delayed. For instance, a transaction that happens in one blockchain gets maliciously repeated in another blockchain. Bitcoin Cash prevents replay attacks using a redefined sighash algorithm.

Bitcoin Cash offers a way to adjust the proof-of-work difficulty quicker than Bitcoin. This is done by adding an "emergency difficulty adjustment" (EDA). Bitcoin has a 2016 block difficulty adjustment interval.

List of Bitcoin Cash Exchanges

The list of exchanges that support Bitcoin Cash are:

- Bittrex
- Kraken
- Cexio
- OKEx
- Houbi
- Korbit
- BtcBox
- Coinfloor
- Changelly
- BTCPOP
- Bitstarex
- Mercado Bitcoin
- ShapeShift
- HitBTC
- Uphold
- Bithumb
- ALFAcashier

- QuadrigaCX
- Evercoin
- Bitcoin Vietnam
- Coinone
- BX.in.th
- SimpleFX
- bitFlyer
- Poloniex
- Binance
- The Rock Trading
- Bitcoin.de

What are the Wallets that support Bitcoin Cash?

The list of wallets that support Bitcoin Cash are:

- Ledger
- Trezor
- KeepKey
- Electron Cash
- Bitcoin.com
- Exodus
- BCC Wallet
- Mobi
- Copay
- Unit
- Web Money

Bitcoin Cash offers quite a few advantages like a more reliable rate of transaction compared to Bitcoin, ease of development (since the code is quite similar to Bitcoin), and lower fees. However, there are concerns about the security of Bitcoin Cash. At any rate, the bottom-line remains that Bitcoin Cash is still new and is yet to prove it's worth.

Chapter 8: Bitcoin Pricing from Launch to Now

What Is Covered In This Chapter?
The important events in Bitcoin history
Bitcoin pricing from launch until now

"There are 3 eras of currency: Commodity based, politically based, and now math based" – Chris Dixon

Bitcoin is less than a decade old. Yet, it has a unique and interesting history. Let us take a look at the important events and pricing of Bitcoin till date.

1. January 3, 2009: The first Bitcoin transaction record, or genesis block, kicked off the Bitcoin blockchain.
2. October 5, 2009: New Liberty Standard opens a service to buy and sell Bitcoin. The initial exchange rate is 1,309.03 BTC to one U.S. Dollar.
3. July 11, 2010: Bitcoin version 0.3 is featured on a popular news and technology website, slashdot.org. Value of Bitcoin surges ten-fold in 5 days, from $0.008 to $0.08.
4. June 1, 2011: The article about the underground website for drugs, Silk Road, is published. Prices increase from $9.21 to $17.61 in a week.

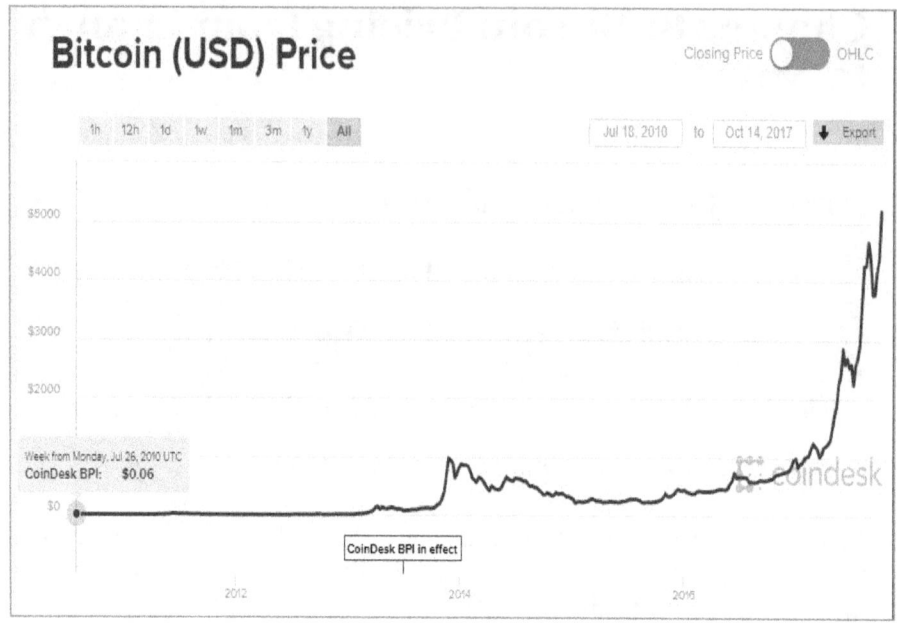

5. March 25, 2013: Cyprus President Nicos Anastasiades orchestrates a bailout, leading to sizable levy collection. Many account holders try to preserve their savings by investing in Bitcoin. Prices increase from $74 to $131 in 10 days.
6. November 18, 20, 2013: The hearing on Bitcoin is held by US Senate. It ended with many of the panelists and Senators agreeing that Bitcoin holds great promise. People' s Bank of China also Okays Bitcoin. Bitcoin value increases from $685 to $1072 in a week and a half.
7. December 5, 2013: Chinese government bans financial institutions from using Bitcoin. The prices decline from $1022 to $839.
8. February 7, 2014: All major exchanges experienced a stoppage of trading due to massive DDoS attacks. Bitcoin prices decline to $547.
9. March 26, 2014: IRS policy document declares Bitcoin to be property, not currency, subject to capital gains tax. Prices decline further to $408.
10. October 22, 2015: The European Court of Justice ruled that the exchange of Bitcoin and "virtual currencies" are not subject to value-added-tax (VAT) in the European

Union. After a series of bad news, this came as welcome respite for Bitcoin. The prices increase to $318 from $274.
11. August 2, 2016: Major Bitcoin exchange, Bitfinex was hacked and $72 million worth Bitcoin were stolen. The Bitcoin price declined 40% following the news and started recovering slowly during the next weeks.
12. November 9, 2016: The historic win of Trump created wild swings in the stock market. This indirectly caused an increase in Bitcoin investors, raising Bitcoin prices from $726 to $1020 in two months.
13. April 1, 2017: Japan recognizes Bitcoin as a legal tender, spurring a price surge. The upcoming Bitcoin fork also lead the cryptocurrency surge from 1085.03 to $2787.
14. August 1, 2017: Bitcoin splits into Bitcoin and Bitcoin Cash. A historic price surge happens from $2787 to $5700.
15. November 8, 2017: Bitcoin surges to $7511 dollars breaking all previous records.

Chapter 9: Investing in Bitcoin and Risk Management

What Is Covered In This Chapter?
Where to buy Bitcoin?
List of Wallets
Pros and Cons of investing in Bitcoin
Risk management: Tips and Techniques

"I think Bitcoins are obviously becoming more and more relevant" –Ashton Kutcher

Every novice investor has a lot of questions about Bitcoins. Here, we will try to address some of the most important ones.

Where to Buy Bitcoins?

There are mainly three ways for buying Bitcoin.

#1 Bitcoin Exchange

Following are a list of different businesses that can help you buy Bitcoin using your bank account.

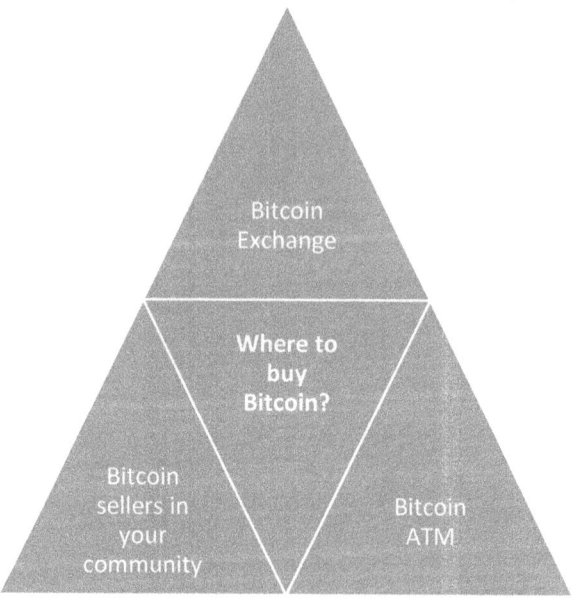

- *International:* Bisq, Bitstamp, Bitwage, Kraken, Local Bitcoins
- *Europe:* AnyCoin Direct, Bitcoin.de, BitPanda, BL3P, Paymium, The Rock Trading
- *Argentina:* SatoshiTango
- *Australia:* Bitcoin Australia, CoinJar, CoinLoft, CoinTree, HardBlock
- *Brazil:* Foxbit, Mercado Bitcoin
- *Cambodia:* Bitcoin Cambodia
- *Canada:* Bitaccess, Canadian Bitcoins, Quadriga CX, QuickBT
- *Chile*: SurBTC
- *China:* Huobi, OKCoin
- *Costa Rica:* BitMae
- *Colombia:* SurBTC
- *India:* Coinsecure, Zebpay
- *Indonesia:* Bitcoin Indonesia
- *Israel:* Bit2C, Bits of Gold
- *Italy:* Postebit
- *Japan:* BtcBox, Coincheck
- *Malaysia:* Luno
- *Mexico:* Volabit
- *Nepal:* Bitsewa
- *New Zealand*: Kiwi-coin
- *Nigeria*: Luno
- *Peru:* SurBTC
- *Poland:* BitBay
- *Singapore:* Luno
- *South Africa:* iceCUBED, Luno
- *South Korea:* Bithumb, Coinone, Korbit
- *Ukraine:* Kuna
- *United Arab Emirates:* BitOasis
- *United Kingdom:* Bittylicious, CoinCorner, Coinfloor
- *United States:* Gemini, itBit
- *Venezuela:* Cryptobuyer

#2 Bitcoin sellers in your community

Websites like Local Bitcoins allow you to exchange your local currency to Bitcoins. These websites allow users to post advertisements stating the exchange rate and payment methods for buying (or selling) Bitcoins. The sellers usually have associated reviews and feedback scores that help buyers choose the best one.

You just need to search and browse through various sellers of Bitcoin in your area, then choose an advertisement that seems suitable for you and reply to it.

Then, you can either agree to meet the person to buy Bitcoins with cash or trade directly with online banking. Bitcoins are placed in the web wallet of the exchange site (e.g.: LocalBitcoins.com) and escrow or transaction services are also provided to protect the buyer of Bitcoins.

#3 Bitcoin ATM

Bitcoin ATMs are similar to a regular ATM, except they allow you to deposit money so that you can buy Bitcoin as well as withdraw money after you sell Bitcoin. You can find the closest Bitcoin ATM using this interactive map of Coin ATM Radar.

The general buy process at the Bitcoin ATMs is as follows:

Step #1: Verification. This is optional and may vary substantially depending on the type of ATM machine. It could either be an SMS code after you enter your mobile number, fingerprint scan, or a scanned copy of your government issued ID proof.

Step #2 Provide the Bitcoin address. The address for depositing Bitcoin can be either entered manually or generated and printed/emailed at the ATM on the fly. It is best to have your own with you before using a machine.

Step #3 Insert cash into the ATM for the purchase.

Step #4 Confirm operation. Once done, the Bitcoins get sent to your Bitcoin address at that moment.

Alternatively, you can also become a Bitcoin miner in order to get Bitcoins. However, to be successful, you would need a high-power computer with a lot of memory and latest hardware.

List of Compatible Bitcoin Wallets

Another question is pertaining to the various types of wallets that are compatible. Here is the list.

Desktop Wallets (Linux, Mac, and Windows):

ArcBit, Armory, Bitcoin Core, Bitcoin Knots, BitGo, Bither, Electrum, GreenAddress, mSIGNA

Hardware Wallets:

DigitalBitbox, KeepKey, Ledger Nano S, Trezor

Mobile Wallets:

For Android: Airbitz, ArcBit, Bither, breadwallet, Coin.Space, Electrum, Green Address, GreenBits, Mycelium, Simple Bitcoin, Bitcoin Wallet

For Blackberry: Bitcoin Wallet

For iOS: Airbitz, ArcBit, Bither, breadwallet, Coin.Space, Green Address

For Windows Phone: Coin.Space

Web Wallets:

BitGo, Coinapult, Coin.Space, Green Address

When considering the risk-reward profile of investing in Bitcoin, it can be compared to investing in a high-risk start-up.

- Just like an early stage start-up, it is possible that Bitcoin will grow exponentially and seize a significant market share of the payments market.
- On the other hand, it is also equally possible that Bitcoin will fail and the invested amount will become zero.

What Are The Advantages Of Investing In Bitcoin?

There are many advantages of investing in Bitcoin.

- ☑ Investing in Bitcoin helps to avoid capital control, confiscation, as well as disproportionate taxation. This is because any Bitcoin user can access his funds as long as he has a device with internet connectivity and a copy of his private keys.
- ☑ Ease of transportation of Bitcoin is a huge positive. The private keys can be uploaded into the cloud or carried in a USB. On the other hand, if you have large amounts of fiat currencies, they are difficult to transport when compared to Bitcoin.
- ☑ Bitcoin has zero storage costs.
- ☑ The record keeping of Bitcoin is done automatically.
- ☑ As the society moves towards cashless payments, Bitcoin's ability to make international money transfers from any smartphone makes it fit nicely into the equation.
- ☑ Alternative currencies are now highly in demand, especially in the emerging markets. Bitcoin still remains the most popular among cryptocurrencies, giving it the first mover advantage.
- ☑ The latest offerings from Bitcoin include prepaid Bitcoin debit cards, Bitcoin peer-to-peer lending, Bitcoin savings accounts, and a range of other services. Many individuals prefer to handle their own money without the need for a bank and Bitcoin provides the perfect solution for this demand.
- ☑ Unlike the physical security of fiat currencies, Bitcoin uses cryptographic security.

What Are The Risks Of Investing In Bitcoin?

Certain risks are also associated with investing in Bitcoin.

- ☒ The code of Bitcoin is open source. This means that it can be easily replicated to form other substitutes.

- As Bitcoin lacks authority such as a central bank to ensure the stability of its value, it has high volatility. Therefore, Bitcoin cannot be used as a store of value.
- Unlike fiat currencies, Bitcoin does not have legal tender status in all countries. This makes it impossible to settle debts with Bitcoin in the respective countries.
- Bitcoin doesn't have any intrinsic value and no physical backing.
- There is no control over the money supply, as it can be changed through a majority process once the miners and users agreeing to the change.
- There is a possibility that Bitcoin will be banned by the government in order to enforce currency controls or prevent illicit uses of cryptocurrencies. Any such negative regulatory changes would have a direct impact Bitcoin prices.
- Unlike commodities like gold, Bitcoin does not have a marginal cost of production to stabilize its price. This means that the down-trends in its price could be acute.
- Unlike bank deposits, there is no deposit insurance for Bitcoin users.
- There are no interest payments given for Bitcoin investment.
- The possibility of 51 percent attack is a major risk of Bitcoin. In case a centralized Bitcoin mining operation gains more than 50% control of the blockchain, no trust would be left in the network.
- The loss of keys or device failure is also a major risk factor.

Possible Scenarios of Bitcoin's Collapse

Following are some scenarios wherein it would fail and the price could collapse.

- Discovery of any serious security flaw which can result in a massive scale of hacking.
- Any attack which undermines the trust in the Bitcoin technology. This could cause users to leave Bitcoin network, prompting a massive sell-off.

- ∅ If another altcoin, metacoin, or payment platform replaces Bitcoin.
- ∅ If there is no internet connectivity or electricity, Bitcoin will not have any value at all.

Bitcoin: Risk Management Techniques

Following are some risk management techniques

1. Reduce the counterparty risk from exchanges by following these guidelines
    a. Thoroughly research the exchange to ensure that it has a solid reputation.
    b. Never leave coins on an exchange when you are not actively trading.
    c. Always trade with only 20-30% of your portfolio.
    d. Diversify your coins across several exchanges
2. Always have an exit strategy in place. For this, you can make use of the support/resistance levels in the chart.
3. Choose techniques based on the market trend. For example, strong trends are best for swing trading while automated scalping works well in a stable market.
4. If you plan to hold your trades for a longer time, use as little leverage as possible. Leverage is basically borrowing or lending an asset. It is always best to close unprofitable positions within 24 hours to avoid paying re-occurring interest.
5. Trade without emotions and remain objective when buying and selling. Avoid the hype and have and clear realistic price target in place.
6. Take care to choose the optimal position size when trading Bitcoin. Position sizing is defined as the dollar value being invested into a particular security (Bitcoin) by an investor.
7. Accept that there would be losses and prepare for it mentally. Remember to never invest more than you can afford to use.
8. Limit the losses by using stop losses. Make sure that you do not set your stop losses too low. This way, you will not lose too much in a single trade.

9. Never trust any service that claims to pay interest on Bitcoins or increase your Bitcoins. This is either extremely risky or an outright scam. If it sounds too good to be true, it usually is! Stay far away from such services.

Despite the risks, investing in Bitcoin has many distinct advantages. By following the risk management techniques outlined, you will be able to maximize profits while minimizing risk from Bitcoin investing.

Chapter 10: Bitcoin Trading

> **What Is Covered In This Chapter?**
> Difference between Bitcoin investing and trading
> Why trade Bitcoin?
> What are the ways to trade Bitcoin?
> The importance of charts
> How to predict future prices using charts?
> Tools, Resources and trading strategies

"Bitcoin is going to change the world from a money transactional standpoint not just for Africa, but for everywhere" - AKON

Bitcoin trading is similar to Bitcoin investing, yet not the same. Here's why.

Bitcoin Investing vs Trading

Bitcoin Investing: Bitcoin investing is a long-term undertaking. It is usually associated with specific goals like portfolio diversification, business or ideological objectives, fiat risk hedging, etc. Bitcoin investors are generally not worried about price volatility. They are less likely to exit their positions unless it is due to some dire eventuality.

Bitcoin Trading: Typically, Bitcoin traders maintain only short-term positions. They stay in a trade for a few hours, or a maximum of few months. Bitcoin traders are price-sensitive. The try to look for a good entry and exit price. Bitcoin traders are quick to close their positions if they don't go in the preferred direction.

Why Trade Bitcoin?

There are quite a few compelling reasons for Bitcoin trading.

Bitcoin has exceptional volatility. This allows for high percentage profits without leveraging. Bitcoin trading is available non-stop; 24 hours a day, 7 days a week. This round-the-clock trading is possible as the volume is distributed across American, European and Asian sessions.

Bitcoin is one of the quickest, cheapest, and most convenient instruments to trade. When compared to other financial instruments, there is a very little barrier to entry for Bitcoin trading. If you own Bitcoins, you can start trading almost instantly.

What Are The Ways to Trade Bitcoin?

Following are the ways to get involved in Bitcoin trading.

As an exchanger: You can join a peer-to-peer exchange marketplace as an exchanger: This doesn't require a lot of financial analysis. You just need to add a spread (say, buying 2% below market price and selling 2% above market price) for making profits.

Sophisticated, high-volume exchanges: Bitcoin exchanges work just like physical currency exchanges. It is best to choose an exchange that offers decent volume and a real-time, responsive trading interface. Examples are Bitfinex, Poloniex, Gemini, GDAX, Kraken, Bitstamp.

Bitcoin Options: Options allow inexpensive hedging of market positions and trading of volatility. There are also many options trading strategies available.

Bitcoin Futures: This contract is usually used as a hedge by people who own a lot of BTC.

Algorithmic trading: This is done by programming a 'bot' with the rules for buying and selling Bitcoins.

CFDs: You can also speculate on Bitcoin's price via fiat-only Contracts for Difference (CFDs).

The Importance of Charts

If you plan to trade Bitcoin, it is imperative that you have a basic understanding of how to read the charts and learn about the various tools for performing technical analysis.

An in-depth explanation about chart reading is currently outside the scope of this book. But here is a quick overview about chart reading.

Charts are created based on two things– price and volume. Each day is represented by a candlestick. A candlestick basically consists of four different parts. They are High price, Low price, Opening price, and Closing price.

The lines at the ends of the candlestick are called **shadow** or **wick**. It indicates the **price action**, or the highest and the lowest price for the day.

The color of a candlestick also holds specific meaning. A **bullish candlestick** would be a white, green, or empty candle with a closing price that is higher than the opening price. On the other hand, a **bearish candlestick** would be a red, black, or filled candle with a closing price that is lesser than the opening price.

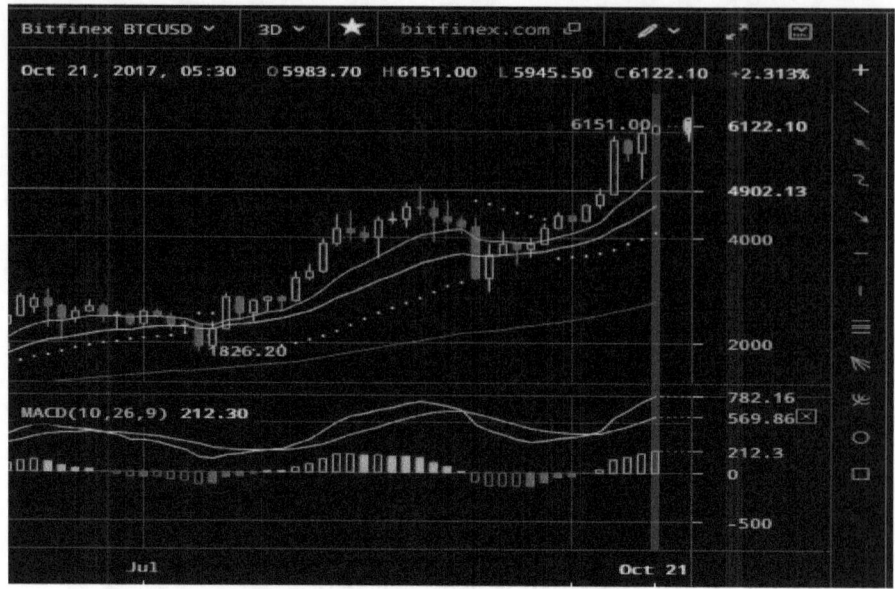

Courtesy: https://cryptowat.ch/bitfinex/btcusd

Predicting Future Prices Using Charts

Charts can be used to predict the future direction and price of Bitcoin. This can be done using candlestick patterns, chart patterns, and technical tools.

#1 Candlestick Patterns

Candlestick patterns basically give a visual insight into the trading psychology of the markets. A **single** candlestick or a combination of **two or more candlesticks** can be used for predicting the bullish as well as bearish trends.
Candlestick patterns are of three types: Neutral, Bullish, and Bearish.

Neutral: A neutral candlestick pattern is called Doji. It has the same open and close price. Based on the length of lower as well as upper shadows, the shape of a Doji can be an inverted cross, a plus sign, or a cross.

Bullish: A bullish candlestick patterns indicate a bullish bias. Some of the important bullish candlestick patterns are Hammer, Bullish engulfing, Piercing Line, Morning Star, Bullish Belt Hold, Bullish Harami, Bullish Harami Cross, Bullish Abandoned baby, and Three White Soldiers.

Bearish: A bearish candlestick patterns indicate a bearish bias. Some of the important bearish candlestick patterns are Bearish engulfing, Bearish Dark Cloud Cover, Bearish Shooting star, Bearish Belt Hold, Bearish Doji Star, Bearish Harami, Bearish Harami Cross, Bearish Abandoned Baby, and Bearish Evening Star.

Candlestick patterns	Chart patterns	Technical tools
Bullish	Bullish	Resistance and Support levels
Bearish	Bearish	Trend lines and trends
Neutral	Continuation	Moving Averages
		Technical Indicators
		Technical Overlays

#2 Chart Patterns

Chart patterns can predict how the market would react once the price breaks free from the specific pattern. An important point to note is that when analyzing the chart patterns, you would not be concerned about the 'Why', or the reason behind it.

There are mainly three types of chart patterns: Bullish Chart patterns, Bearish Chart Patterns, and Continuation Chart Patterns.

Bullish Patterns: A bullish pattern indicates a trend reversal from bearish to a bullish bias. The important bullish chart patterns are Bullish Inverted Head and Shoulders,

Bullish Rounding Bottom Patterns, Bullish Double Bottom Patterns, and Bullish Triple Bottom Patterns.

Bearish Patterns: A bearish pattern indicates a trend reversal from bullish to a bearish bias. The important bearish chart patterns are Bearish Head and Shoulders Pattern, Bearish Rounding Top Pattern, Bearish Double Top Pattern, and Bearish Triple Top Pattern.

Continuation Patterns: Whenever continuation patterns are formed during an uptrend, the uptrend would continue to be prevalent for some more time. Similarly, whenever continuation patterns are formed during a downtrend, the downtrend would continue for some more time. The important continuation patterns are Continuation Rectangle Patterns, Continuation Triangle Patterns, and Continuation Flag Patterns.

#3 Technical Tools

The main tools of Technical Analysis are Resistance and Support levels, Trend lines and trends, Moving Averages, Technical Indicators, and Overlays.

Resistance and Support levels: Support refers to the level of the price at which there is a *strong demand*. The strength of this demand would prevent the price from moving further downwards. Resistance basically refers to the price levels wherein the sellers are very strong and there is a high supply available. Hence, the price would be prevented from raising higher than this level.

Trend lines and trends: Trend lines are basically straight lines formed by connecting two or more price points of a chart and then extrapolated into the future. There are basically two types of trend lines: uptrend line and downtrend line.

Courtesy: *https://Bitcoincharts.com/charts/bitstampUSD*

Moving Averages: Moving averages are used for smoothing over the price actions so that its overall trend can be made visible. They are plotted using the previous prices and hence would have a lag. There are mainly two types of moving averages: Simple Moving Average (SMA) and Exponential Moving Average (EMA).

Technical Indicators: The important Technical Indicators are RSI, MACD, Stochastic, A/D Line, and CCI.

Technical Overlays: The important Overlays are Bollinger Bands and Price Channels.

Tools and Resources for Bitcoin Trading

- Cryptowatch, Bitcoin Charts, and Bitcoin Wisdom: Provides Live price charts of all major Bitcoin exchanges.
- Bitcoinmarkets – This is a sub-reddit on Bitcoin trading. New users can use this space to ask questions and receive guidance on trading techniques and strategy.

- TradingView – This is a trading community. There are also good trading charts and ideas.

Bitcoin Trading Strategies

Following are some trading strategies for Bitcoin.

Buy and Hold: Also called 'holders', they are not worried about the daily price fluctuations and even extreme price moves. Holders consider price crashes as an opportunity to acquire more coins at a lower price. They may take profits if they believe the price has reached an unsustainable peak. However, they are not unlikely to liquidate their entire position.

Note that this strategy is not best for CFDs due to the unnecessary and unjustifiable cost of daily premium that is required to hold CFDs over the long term. There is also an increased risk of keeping the simulated Bitcoins on an exchange when compared to keeping the real Bitcoins under your personal control.

Swing Trading: Here, the trader maintains his position for a few days to several months with the aim to trade significant price moves between two extremes. Swing traders usually use indicators like the RSI (Relative Strength Index), Bollinger Bands, and the Stochastic Oscillator.

Swing trading is well suited for CFDs due to the ideal timeframe and the fact that larger price moves will amply compensate for the spread and Premium.

Trend Trading: Here, there is no specific target in mind for the trader. They follow the trend until clear reversal signs ensue. The momentum indicators like the ROC (Rate of Change) and MACD (Moving Average Convergence-Divergence) is used for identifying the trend as early as possible.

Trend trading is also well-suited for CFDs.

Day trading: These are full-time traders who use hourly or sub-hourly charts with occasional reference to higher timeframes for entering and exiting trades. Day trading is well suited with CFDs except for the times of low volatility when the price action is flat.

Scalping: Every small move is used by scalpers for making small, but frequent profits. They usually use charts of 5-minute duration or less. Scalping is entirely unsuited to CFDs due to the spread, which pushes trading fees above expected returns.

Chapter 11: The Security Aspect of Bitcoin

> **What Is Covered In This Chapter?**
>
> Why Bitcoin network is secure?
>
> What is 51% attack?
>
> How to secure wallet – two factor authentication, multi sig, mnemonic codes
>
> Tips to stay vigilant

"Don't store coins on exchanges! Bitcoin users have lost over $1 billion worth of Bitcoins in exchange hacks and scams." - Jordan Tuwiner

One of the biggest concerns of investors is regarding the security aspect of the Bitcoin ecosystem. According to media reports, Bitcoin network and protocol have been hacked many times in the past years. But this is quite inaccurate.

The hacks occurred due to the flaw in the security of the associated services built on top of the Bitcoin network, such as wallet providers and exchanges. Bitcoin network hasn't been hacked successfully yet, nor is it likely to happen.

Why Is Bitcoin Network Secure?

Bitcoin is a decentralized network, which means that it cannot be hacked in the traditional sense of the word. Each individual user ensures there is no central point of failure. Even if all users of the USA get hacked at the same time, the Bitcoin network will still stay undisturbed.

Due to the strong cryptography used by the Bitcoin network, it would require the combined processing powers of all supercomputers in existence today and millions of years to even have a small chance of breach in the Bitcoin network. Cryptography is a technique for secure communication in the presence of third parties, using long sequences of un-guessable secret codes.

Every Bitcoin wallet address is protected using a private key. This key cannot be known by anyone other than the users. The only way that the key would be found is if the computer or mobile device in which Bitcoin wallet software is installed is compromised.

The presence of dedicated Bitcoin nodes also strengthens the security of Bitcoin network. Every Bitcoin node is a device like a computer, mobile device etc. that hosts the entire Bitcoin blockchain since the genesis block. These nodes verify the integrity, neutrality, and chronological order of all Bitcoin transactions from the genesis block till now.

There is, however, the possibility that the Bitcoin platforms may get hacked. This is because Bitcoin services or platforms (as opposed to the whole Bitcoin network itself) relies on one or more centralized servers.

Bitcoin exchanges are services built on top of the blockchain in a centralized manner. However, no direct connection exists between the Bitcoin network and any Bitcoin service in existence today. A Bitcoin wallet is the only connection between users and the blockchain and they too, are layered on top of the blockchain.

Interaction or alteration of the Bitcoin blockchain is not possible for individual users as well as Bitcoin services. The function of Bitcoin services is to broadcast certain types of transactions to the Bitcoin network. In case the transactions never get relayed, the Bitcoin network will simply continue working as before. Similarly, even if an individual user gets hacked, it wouldn't disrupt the Bitcoin network at all.

The only thing that can do irreparable harm to the Bitcoin network is something called the 51 percent attack, which is quite unlikely to happen.

What is 51 Percent Attack?

When an organization or users are somehow able to control (hypothetically) the majority of the network mining power or hashrate, it gives rise to a potential attack called 51% attack.

Bitcoin's security rests on the concept that all miners would agree on a shared ledger called the blockchain. In order to verify what they are working on, is the valid blockchain, Bitcoin nodes look to each other.

Now, if the majority of miners (more than 50%) are controlled by a single entity, they may attempt to influence which transactions should get approval. They can also prevent other transactions and allow their own coins to be spent multiple times. This process is called double spending.

If 51% attack takes place successfully, the confidence on Bitcoin and the value of Bitcoin as a currency would plummet.

51% attack doesn't give full power over Bitcoin network because the attacker can only modify the transactions of the latest few blocks and only create coins as mining rewards. With the current network mining difficulty levels, large-scale governments, let alone mining pools would not be able to easily mount a 51% attack.

Securing Your Wallet

Before we delve into the security aspects of Bitcoin wallets, let us recap a little about public and private keys.

For the sake of simplicity, let us assume Bitcoin to be locked within invisible vaults. Bitcoin is technically never moved between the addresses. Instead, it always sits within these vaults.

When Dave makes a simple Bitcoin transaction to Andrew, this is what happens: Dave removes his lock from the Bitcoin vault and Andrew places his lock instead. Now, the lock is the 'public key' while the key to unlocking the lock is the 'Private key'.

Dave basically uses his private key to unlock the lock. Since a copy of the lock of Andrew is available for everybody, it is easy to encrypt anything for Andrew. This just means that Dave can lock Andrew's Bitcoin for him. However, for unlocking the lock, Andrew would need his 'Private key'.

Now, the interesting fact about Bitcoin is that it has a built-in scripting language. This allows you to design all kinds of locks. This is what makes the Bitcoin wallet more secure.

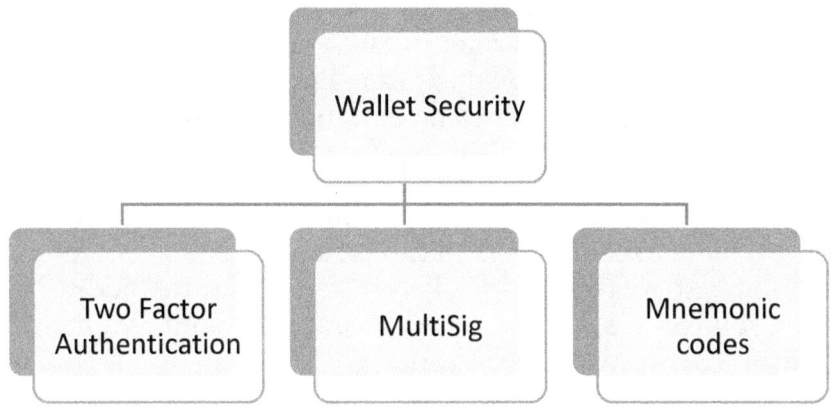

Two Factor Authentication: Two Factor Authentication (2FA) provides an extra layer of security for your Bitcoin. It is a process wherein you have to verify your identity using two forms of authentication. Many Bitcoin wallets provide 2FA. For transactions, you must use your regular password in combination with a text message (SMS message), Google Authenticator, Yubikey, or Email.

MultiSig: This is short for Multi-signature. Any standard Bitcoin transaction requires just one signature – of the owner of the private key associated with the Bitcoin address. But MultiSig requires multiple signatures to authorize. The Bitcoin multisignature addresses usually have 3 associated private keys and some have the capability to have a maximum of 15 associated private keys. For authorizing a transaction, 2 out of 3 key holders are required.

Multisig is particularly useful in case of business partnerships. Assume that Ron, Marie and Peter open a business together and want to invest their money. But nobody wants a single person to have the private keys to their pooled money. So each of them gets a key and then they use a multisig wallet that requires 2 out of the 3 keys. The money remains safe, yet quickly accessible.

The biggest advantage of having a multisig wallet is that your Bitcoin wouldn't be lost in case you lose one private key.

Mnemonic codes: Mnemonic codes are necessary for recovering your Bitcoin wallet in case you forget your login information. Mnemonic code or mnemonic sentence is a group of easy to remember words. The mnemonic passphrase is provided to you when you sign up for the Wallet.

There are two steps: generating the mnemonic and converting it into a binary seed. This seed can be later used to generate deterministic wallets using BIP-0032 or similar methods. When you recover your wallet with your mnemonic, your password will be displayed to you.

Tips to Stay Vigilant and Avoid Scams

As the price of Bitcoin surged, so did the number of scams related to Bitcoin. Scammers typically target new Bitcoin users, especially those who are less tech-savvy users. Follow these tips to avoid Bitcoin scams.

Choose an Exchange after researching it well: Always study your intended exchange very well to make sure that it is trustworthy. Read through the reviews of users who have already used the exchange and search forums like Reddit for user comments and experiences. If your intended exchange is not listed on at least a few review sites, it is possible that it may be a scam.

Check Seller Feedback: In many peer-to-peer exchanges like Wall of Coins and LocalBitcoins, seller's feedback is usually listed. Your trade is likely to go through without hassle in case you choose sellers whose feedback is mostly positive. It is best to stay away from sellers with a lot of negative rating and find another reliable seller.

Make Use of Escrow: The general approach of a scammer is to request you to send Bitcoins and assure that they will pay you via PayPal as soon as they receive the Bitcoin. Never agree to such a trade because Bitcoin payments are irreversible. Once you send Bitcoin first, the scammer can simply not pay you and keep their Bitcoins. PayPal also cannot help you with the dispute. This is because of the pseudonymous nature of Bitcoin which doesn't record the identity of a sender or recipient.

Always Triple Check Bitcoin the Address: A Bitcoin address is basically an identifier representing the destination or origin for a Bitcoin transaction. You can create new or additional Bitcoin addresses free of charge through the installed Bitcoin software, or you can obtain a Bitcoin wallet address from an exchange or online wallet provider. All this does not require an active Internet connection.

Every Bitcoin address is case sensitive and exact and is between 26 and 35 alphanumeric characters in length. Changing the case would result in an invalid recipient address, and the funds would not be transferred. There is also spam software that replaces the actual Bitcoin address by another similar-looking address. To avoid losing your money and Bitcoin, make sure to triple check the Bitcoin address before authorizing any transaction.

Backups: Perform regular backups of a Bitcoin wallet in order to protect against theft, computer failure, and human error. However, make sure that you never store them online. In addition to all this, always use at least a 16 digit password and use the latest version of the Bitcoin software.

The Bitcoin network is a quite secure network. By securing your wallet properly and staying vigilant, you can easily avoid theft and scams.

Chapter 12: Bitcoin Transactions for Business

What Is Covered In This Chapter?
Why Bitcoin is a good payment option for businesses?

"Bitcoin will remain, in my opinion, a relentless anomaly that refuses to go away – a black swan that cannot be ignored or extinguished" –Andreas Antonopoulos

Bitcoin has unique features that make it an inexpensive and a secure way for making business payments. Let's see why.

Why Bitcoin Is a Good Payment Option for Businesses

The following features makes Bitcoin is a good payment option for businesses.

Low fees: In order to receive Bitcoins, there are no fees to be paid. Even when spending Bitcoins, many wallets let you control how much fees should be paid. Wallets usually have quite reasonable default fees, though higher fees can help in getting faster confirmation of your transactions. The best part is that the amount transferred and the fees for the amount have no correlation. It is possible to send 50,000 Bitcoins for the same fees as sending one Bitcoin.

Protection against Payment Reversals: Businesses that accept PayPal or credit cards face the problem of payments that are reversed later. The cost of such fraud leads to increased prices and limited market reach, which in turn penalizes customers. Since Bitcoin payments are irreversible as well as secure, there would be no more of such cost of fraud.

Quicker international payments: Businesses don't have to wait for 2-3 business days for payments to go through, check the banking holidays, or calculate the additional fees for international money transfer. Sending Bitcoins internationally is quite easy and there are no special limitations on the maximum amount or minimum that businesses can send.

Multi-signature: Additional features like multisig ensure that the Bitcoins can be spent only if a certain number of people authorize the transaction. For a business board of directors, this is quite a blessing as they can not only prevent unauthorized expenditures but also track which members permitted each payment.

Transparency: Bitcoin provides complete transparency. This is quite useful in the case of non-profit organizations as they can let the public see how much they receive in donations.

No need for PCI compliance: Credit cards need excessive security checks in order to comply with the PCI standard to be accepted online. Although Bitcoin needs businesses to secure their payment requests and wallets, businesses will save on the costs and responsibilities that come with processing sensitive information like credit card numbers from their customers.

Get more business and visibility: Since Bitcoin is still an emerging market, many new customers are searching for ways to spend their Bitcoins. If businesses start accepting Bitcoin payments, it will not only attract customers but also increase visibility, especially for online businesses.

Chapter 13: FOMO/FUD

> **What Is Covered In This Chapter?**
>
> **What is FUD?**
>
> **What is FOMO?**

"Bitcoin is hard-coded to be limited, it's like a collectible"

— Bobby Lee

When trading or learning about Bitcoin, two terminologies that you would invariably come across are FOMO and FUD. Here is a brief overview about them.

What is FUD?

F.U.D stands for Fear, Uncertainty, and Doubt. Anything that intends to instill fear, uncertainty, or doubts in Bitcoin in order to dissuade people from it is called FUD.

For example, making outrageous claims, twisting of facts, and even outright attack on the security of Bitcoin are some ways in which FUD is tried to be instilled in Bitcoin users. Many try this tactic so that people wouldn't use Bitcoin and only use government-authorized money like dollars.

In recent times, FUD is seen to be used by many cryptocurrency communities. Users of certain cryptocurrencies try to leverage FUD-like tactics in order to make the other cryptocurrencies appear inferior or flawed and promote their own preferred currency over others.

What is FOMO?

FOMO stands for Fear Of Missing Out. It is basically the apprehension that others might be having rewarding experiences with Bitcoin investing while you lose out on excellent opportunities.

Many financial experts believe that the current Bitcoin frenzy is mostly driven by FOMO. The psychological fear that they will be missing out on the next Bitcoin surge is causing investors to queue up to invest in Bitcoin, even with their life savings. However, even a slight dip in the Bitcoin prices creates panic, leading to a sell-off. This cycle starts again when the prices start to increase after the dip.

The only way to win in Bitcoin investment is to invest the money you can afford to lose, and then hold on to the investment for a long time.

Chapter 14: Dollar Cost Averaging

> **What Is Covered In This Chapter?**
>
> **What is Dollar Cost Averaging?**
>
> **How does it work?**

Bitcoin is the beginning of something great: a currency without a government, something necessary and imperative" — Nassim Taleb

One of the common problems with investing a lump sum in Bitcoin is that it may be invested at a wrong time. For example, assume that a newbie invested all his money at point (A) in the chart. Then, he may panic and sell his holdings when the price of Bitcoin declined and reached point (B). This would cause him to miss out on the surge in price that happened at point (C).

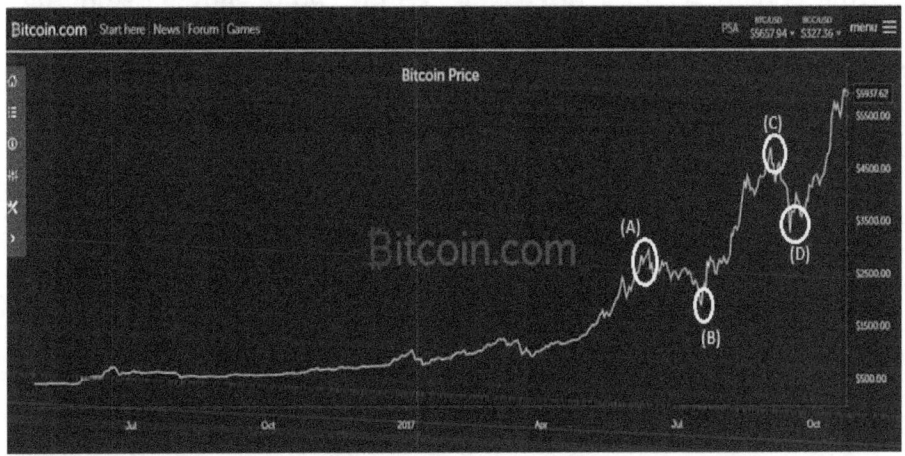

The solution for this is something called Dollar Cost Averaging.

What is Dollar Cost Averaging?

Every investor wants to 'time the market' and buy low and sell high. But this may not be practical in many scenarios, even if it is based on the sophisticated technical indicators, latest news, or government data.

Dollar Cost Averaging is a great way to make sure that you are not paying a high price for the purchase of Bitcoin. It is a simple technique that involves making fixed, regular investments to accumulate wealth over time.

How Does Dollar Cost Averaging Work?

If you plan to invest $500 in Bitcoin per month, you can invest $100 into Bitcoin every week. In case the price of the digital currency falls, your weekly $100 will buy you more Bitcoin. In case the Bitcoin price rises, your weekly investment will buy you less Bitcoin. But your monthly average cost for purchasing Bitcoin would be lower when you pay it this way.

Bitcoin has high volatility, leading to major price swings. So, Dollar Cost Averaging helps you to sell or buy Bitcoin such that you get a better price when compared to selling or buying it at once.

Investing via Dollar Cost Averaging also helps in relieving pressure to find the perfect point to enter and exit.

For example, if you follow this strategy of Dollar Cost Averaging and invest your money at point (A), (B), (C) and (D) in the above chart, you will get higher returns when compared to investing the entire amount at say, point (C).

Chapter 15: Bitcoin Mutual Funds

What Is Covered In This Chapter?
List of funds
Approach
Who invests in crypto funds?

"Bitcoin is cash with wings" — Charlie Shrem

One of the best ways to minimize risks from Bitcoin is to invest in funds that track cryptocurrencies. In the recent times, many cryptocurrency funds have soared in value compared to traditional assets. In 2017, 84 crypto hedge funds have already been launched. Here are a few important ones.

List of Funds

Grayscale Bitcoin Investment Trust

Grayscale Bitcoin Investment Trust (GBTC) is a fund run by Barry Silbert of the Digital Currency Group (DCG). GBTC shares trade at a premium when compared purchasing Bitcoin traditionally through an exchange and have gained 220.59% this year. As GBTC is publicly quoted, it is one of the easier ways for investors to get exposure to Bitcoin. GBTC can be purchased through traditional self-directed IRAs.

BK Capital Management

Created by CNBC host and investment analyst Brian Kelly, the BKCM investment asset fund focuses on "liquid exchange" digital assets. BKCM was up 68% in April and 172% YTD and has a Bitcoin allocation of 50% to 85%.

Ark Investment Management

Ark Innovation (ARKK) invests in innovative companies, technologies as well as funds like GBTC. ARKK has four ETF's available. They are Industrial Innovation ETF, Web x.0 ETF, Genomic Revolution Multi-Sector ETF, and the Innovation ETF.

Self-Directed IRAs

There are many self-directed IRAs available. California-based Bitcoin IRA Company allows the purchase of BTC with traditional IRAs or a 401K. Some other companies include the Millennium Trust, Entrust Group, and Pensco.

Approach

The approach of each crypto fund is also different. For instance, market-neutral funds offered by the London-based BitSpread trades on price differentials while many others bet on new coins issued to raise funds via initial coin offerings (ICOs) and price direction.

Who Invests In Crypto Funds?

Due to the pronounced price swings in cryptocurrency, many of the pension funds, insurance companies, and large mutual funds across the globe are currently hesitant to invest in these funds. There are also liquidity concerns. In addition, most of these funds are currently worth between $5 million to $20 million range which is well below the threshold most institutional investors would consider.

For now, the ones investing in crypto funds are companies managing money for wealthy families, high-net-worth individuals, private wealth managers, and some venture capital investors.

Conclusion

Bitcoin is taking the world by storm, thanks to its innovative idea and unique features. It is currently the most liquid and widely accepted cryptocurrency in the world.

This book is intended as a beginners guide to Bitcoin and I have included all the important aspects of Bitcoin, right from its origin and history. I hope this book was able to help you understand the basics of the #1 cryptocurrency, Bitcoin.

Remember that Bitcoin is still evolving and rapid strides are taking place in the technology even as you read this line.

I hope this book inspires you to learn more about Bitcoin and keep up with the latest advancements.

Thank you and good luck!

If you enjoyed this book please leave an honest review.

"Bitcoin is exciting because it shows how cheap it can be. Bitcoin is better than currency in that you don´t have to be physically in the same place and, of course, for large transactions, currency can get pretty inconvenient" – Bill Gates

FREE eBook Available
This is my FREE GIFT to YOU

Go to the link below to collect your FREE GIFT & Avoid the 5 Deadly Mistakes

http://eepurl.com/c9Lsr9

www.ingramcontent.com/pod-product-compliance
Lightning Source LLC
Chambersburg PA
CBHW070312230526
45470CB00002B/837